FISHING SPIDERS

SPIDERS DISCOVERY LIBRARY

Jason Cooper

Rourke

Publishing LLC

Vero Beach, Florida 32964

www.rourkepublishing.com
1-800-394-7055
Vero Beach Florida

PHOTO CREDITS: Cover, p. 4 © James H. Carmichael; title page, p. 6, 10, 22 © Francesco Tomasinelli; p. 7, 8, 11, 12, 15, 16, 19, 20 © Lynn M. Stone

Title page: *A young fishing spider rows across water using its legs as oars.*

Editor: Frank Sloan

Cover and interior design by Nicola Stratford

Library of Congress Cataloging-in-Publication Data

Cooper, Jason, 1942-
 Fishing spiders / Jason Cooper.
   p. cm. -- (Spiders discovery)
 Includes bibliographical references.
 ISBN 1-59515-446-9 (hardcover)
 1. Dolomedes--Juvenile literature. I. Title.
 QL458.42.P5C66 2006
 595.4'4--dc22
                          2005010727

Printed in the USA

CG/CG

Table of Contents

Fishing Spiders

Fishing spiders have a special skill among spiders. They catch, kill, and eat fish. Don't think trophy fish, or even many fish, though. Fishing spiders catch very small fish. And they catch far more insects than fish. But the fact that a spider catches fish at all is very unusual.

Fishing spiders are a small group within a larger family of spiders, the nursery web spiders. Like all spiders, they are **arachnids**.

A fishing spider holds its fish prey in leg-like pedipalps.

At home on and in water, fishing spiders can run on a water surface. They have tiny hairs on the tips of their legs. The hairs repel water, so they act like tiny corks. Fishing spiders can dive, too, and stay under water for several minutes.

Fishing spiders step lightly on the water and don't sink!

A nursery web spider guards its web in a Florida marsh.

Fishing spiders have been known to dive to a depth of 7 inches (18 centimeters). Doesn't sound like much? It's like a 40-foot (12-meter) dive for an adult man!

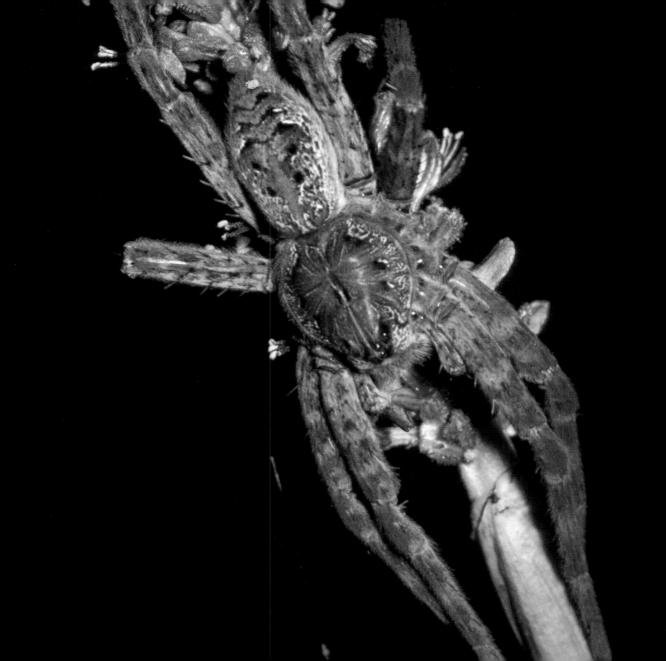

Predator and Prey

Fishing spiders don't always eat fish, nor do they always hunt in water. They often hunt among the plants near a body of water. There they wait. When **prey** comes within range, the fishing spider rushes toward it.

A fishing spider hunting on the pond surface feels even slight vibrations. They tell the spider something about the size and location of what made the vibration.

The fishing spider may chase prey on the water surface. Prey is often an insect that has fallen into the water.

A fishing spider hugs a pickerel-weed stem.

A fishing spider bites its prey and injects it with **venom**. The venom paralyzes and kills the prey.

Different kinds of fishing spiders hunt either by day or night. At least some species, including the common six-spotted fishing spider, are **predators** by day and night. Fishing spiders sometimes become prey for frogs, fish, and birds.

A European fishing spider clings to a minnow with her pedipalps.

A fishing spider and its spiky legs step through plant stems.

Fish actually make up a small part of a fishing spider's diet. These spiders eat insects and other small animals, including a tadpole now and then.

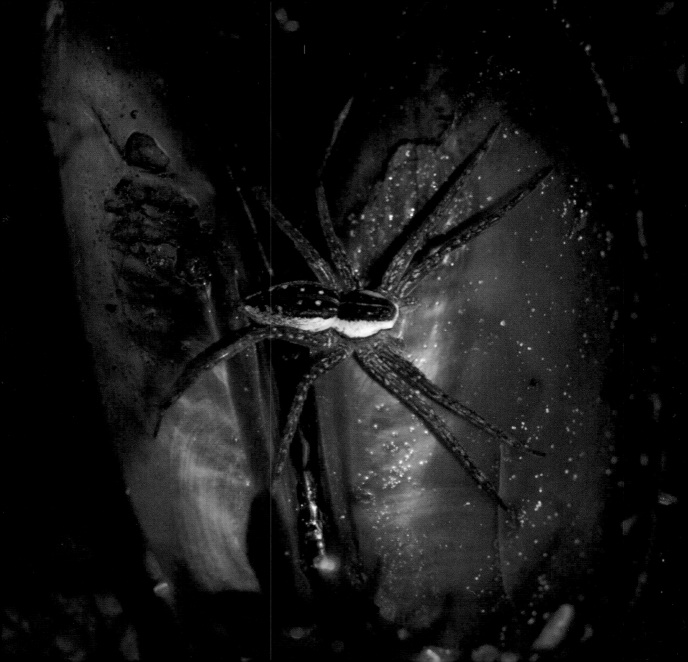

What Fishing Spiders Look Like

Fishing spiders are large, often hairy spiders with 8 eyes. Most fishing spiders are about 1 inch (2.5 centimeters) in length. In some species, the female is much larger than the male.

Fishing spiders tend to be brown, gray, white, and black. In many ways, including color, they are similar to wolf spiders.

The earth colors of a freshwater clamshell match a six-spotted fishing spider's.

Like all spiders, fishing spiders have two main body parts. The **abdomen** is the longer, thicker part of the body. It holds the heart, silk glands, lungs, and other organs. The **cephalothorax** includes the spider's head, brain, mouth, and much of the stomach.

The fishing spider's forward section is the cephalothorax.

Where Fishing Spiders Live

Arachnologists believe nearly 300 species of nursery web spiders live throughout the world. About 15 species live in North America, north of Mexico. About 10 of those species, in the group *Dolomedes*, are fishing spiders.

Fishing spiders are common around ponds, streams, swamps, and boat docks. They like dark places under plant leaves, beneath bridges, and in big roadside pipes.

The dark underside of a leaf suits a fishing spider just fine.

The Fishing Spider's Life Cycle

Nursery web and fishing spiders lay eggs and put them in silk **egg sacs**. Some egg sacs have at least 1,400 eggs.

The fishing spider first carries the egg sac in her jaws. But as the eggs' hatching time nears, she spins a silk web. It is this habit for which nursery web spiders are named.

A nursery web spider carries her egg sac to a nursery web.

In the northern states and Canada, a fishing spider lays eggs between June and September.

Woven among leaves, the spider's web protects the egg sac. It is also a nursery for the babies, known as spiderlings.

The mother fishing spider guards the nursery for about one week, or until the spiderlings crawl out. Baby spiders look like tiny copies of their parents.

A nursery web protects a spider's eggs and young.

Fishing Spiders and People

Fishing spiders are large enough to bite a person. But it is not a likely event. Fishing spider bites are uncomfortable but not dangerous— unless you're a fish.

Like all spiders, fishing spiders help keep insect populations in check. They play an important role in keeping nature's balance.

Fishing spiders help keep a healthy balance between hunters and their prey.

Glossary

abdomen (AB duh mun) — the second major part of a spider's body; the section that holds heart, lungs, silk glands, and other organs

arachnids (uh RAK nidz) — spiders and their kin; boneless, eight-legged animals with two major body parts and no wings or antennas

arachnologists (uh RAK nol uh jists) — scientists who study arachnids

cephalothorax (SEF uh luh THOR aks) — the body section of a spider that includes such organs as eyes, brain, venom glands, and sucking stomach

egg sacs (EGG SAKS) — cases or containers, usually ball-shaped, for eggs

predators (PRED uh turz) — animals that hunt other animals for food

prey (PRAY) — an animal that is hunted by another animal for food

venom (VEN um) — poison produced by certain animals, largely to kill or injure prey

Index

Further Reading

Miller, Jake. *Fishing Spiders.* Powerkids Press, 2004
Simon, Seymour. *Spiders.* HarperCollins, 2003

Websites To Visit

www.fcps.k12.va.us/StratfordLandingES/Ecology/mpages/six-spottedfishingspider.htm
www.uark.edu/depts/entomolo/museum/dolomede.html
www.americanarachnology.org/

About The Author

Jason Cooper has written several children's books about a variety of topics for Rourke Publishing, including the recent series *Animals Growing Up* and *Fighting Forces*.